Original title:
Propagation and Poetry

Copyright © 2025 Creative Arts Management OÜ
All rights reserved.

Author: Amelia Montgomery
ISBN HARDBACK: 978-1-80581-855-7
ISBN PAPERBACK: 978-1-80581-382-8
ISBN EBOOK: 978-1-80581-855-7

Fertile Imaginations

In a garden where thoughts grow wild,
Every idea, like a playful child.
They bounce around on the fertile ground,
In the soil of nonsense, joy is found.

Seeds of laughter, planted with glee,
Sprouting jokes like a flowering tree.
Each thought a petal, bright and bold,
In the orchard of humor, stories unfold.

Budding Expressions

Tiny phrases peek out to play,
Twisting their tongues in a merry way.
Words frolic freely, not keeping score,
Budding expressions demand an encore!

With a tickle of wit and a splash of rhyme,
They dance in the sunshine, oh so sublime.
Each giggle a blossom, each chuckle a sprout,
In this whimsical world, joy's never in doubt.

Lines in the Landscape

Lines meander like rivers in jest,
Winding through meadows, they never rest.
They laugh with the daisies, tickle the trees,
In this canvas of chaos, they move with ease.

Sketching the moments, both silly and spry,
Chasing the clouds as they drift by.
Each curve a giggle, each dot a cheer,
In the artwork of chatter, amusement is near.

Blossom Beneath the Ink

In the depths of the notebook, ideas sprout,
Like daisies dancing, never a doubt.
With a wink of a pen, they flirt and play,
Unfolding mishaps in a colorful way.

Underneath layers of scribbled delight,
Funny tales blossom, brushing off fright.
Laughter emerges from ink's gentle grasp,
Creating a bouquet of joy you can clasp.

A Symphony of Seasons

Winter's chill sings a tune,
Snowflakes dance like a cartoon.
Spring arrives with a giggle,
Blossoms bloom, laughter wiggle.

Summer's sun plays hide and seek,
Ice cream melts, oh what a streak!
Autumn leaves do a funny waltz,
Squirrels chuckle, no time to false.

Petals and Prose

Daisies wearing silly hats,
Bumblebees talk like chitchat.
Words tumble like a garden snail,
Witty puns on a flowery trail.

Tulips whisper jokes so bright,
They bloom in laughter with delight.
Each petal a phrase of cheer,
Spreading smiles far and near.

Echoes of the Earth

Mountains laugh in playful tones,
Rivers tickle their own stones.
Trees chat with a breezy sigh,
Nature's humor soaring high.

Clouds roll by with a cheeky grin,
Droplets fall like a playful kin.
The soil giggles with delight,
As flowers bloom, oh what a sight!

Verses in Bloom

Roses rhyme with a fragrant twist,
Silly sonnets that can't be missed.
Each bud a line, freshness abounds,
Witty verses sprouting from grounds.

Garden gnomes penning their plays,
In the sun's bright, whimsical rays.
Nature's laughter, a grand refrain,
In every petal, joy remains.

Nature's Narrative

In the garden, seeds do dance,
Worms wear shoes, given the chance.
Sunflowers giggle, stretching high,
While bees buzz jokes that fly by.

The trees whisper tales so bright,
Of squirrels who argue, quite the sight.
Rabbits play cards under the moon,
While fireflies flicker, humming a tune.

The Cultivated Spirit

There's a plant with a penchant for sass,
It throws shade like a cheeky class.
Roses wear crowns, feeling so grand,
While daisies debate who's the best in the land.

The pumpkins joke, 'We're squashin' the game!'
As carrots claim fame in the veggie hall of fame.
Mint loves to gossip, flavors so bold,
While the basil rolls its eyes watching it unfold.

Inked in the Meadow

In the meadow, ink spills with flair,
As butterflies flutter, unaware.
A poet's quill turns flowers to words,
While grasshoppers mimic cool nerds.

Each daffodil dreams of being a star,
While crickets chirp, 'Have you gone too far?'
Dandelions giggle, blowing their seeds,
Creating wish clouds, fulfilling all needs.

Flourishing Lines

In lines of green, the verses grow,
With cacti sharing tales of woe.
Sunshine tickles the playful leaves,
While laughter rings, and joy believes.

Frogs croak sonnets, a froggy delight,
And peacocks strut, it's a colorful sight.
Weeds crack jokes about being too free,
While flowers whisper, 'Who'll water me?'

Dreams on the Vine

In the garden where giggles grows,
Dreams hang like grapes in a row.
With every pluck, a chuckle spills,
Juicy thoughts offer sweet thrills.

Sunshine tickles the leaves' green faces,
While bumblebees dance in their places.
A rhyme plops down like a ripe fruit,
Making each moment delightfully cute.

Tapestry of Tendrils

Twists and turns of laughter unfold,
Tendrils weaving tales of bold.
A yarn spun from fluff and jest,
In this maze, we're all a guest.

Wiggly words float like balloons,
Swaying to the tune of silly tunes.
Each line embroidered with a grin,
A tapestry where fun begins.

Harmony in the Hedges

In hedges thick with whispers sweet,
Funny critters gather to meet.
A squirrel recites, a rabbit snorts,
As hedgehogs share their awkward shorts.

With each giggle, the blooms all sway,
Nature's chorus in a delightful play.
Though roots tangle and branches tease,
Laughter echoes through the leaves with ease.

Harvesting Words

Gather words like apples bright,
With baskets full, we take to flight.
Each pluck is a pun, a witty twist,
In this orchard, joy cannot be missed.

With every chuckle, the branches bend,
Beneath the sun, our laughter sends.
A crop of rhymes, a garden grown,
In fields of fun, we've brightly sown.

The Language of Growth

In the garden, worms do chat,
Wiggling tales beneath the mat.
Seeds debate their sprouty fate,
While flowers gossip at a great rate.

Roses blush when daisies tease,
Bumblebees sing with such ease.
Nature's jokes fly through the air,
Even cacti laugh without a care.

Echoes in the Garden

In the breeze, the leaves converse,
Whispering secrets, oh so terse.
Sunlight chuckles at the shade,
While daisies in the sun parade.

Gnomes make puns, they stand so still,
Plenty of humor by the hill.
Jumping beans with jigs they show,
Keeping spirits high, you know!

Stanzas of the Soil

Underfoot, the roots compose,
A symphony where laughter grows.
Earthworms twirl, they find their beat,
Tap-dancing 'neath the farmer's feet.

Compost piles turn jokes with flair,
While mushrooms joke about their hair.
Nuts in shells crack wise and loud,
All join in—what a goofy crowd!

Rhythms of Renewal

Spring arrives, the crocs sing bright,
Promising fungi, quite a sight.
Pollinators in a raucous race,
Buzzing with jokes, a buzzing place.

So while the buds break from the ground,
Laughter lingers all around.
Each petal's joke, a bright confetti,
Nature's humor, always ready!

The Language of Growth

In a garden where plants twist and dance,
Words sprout wings, given half a chance.
A tomato once whispered, 'I'm ripe for rhyme!'
While daisies debate how to tell time.

They giggle and chatter, all green and spry,
Bright sunflowers raise their heads to the sky.
Lettuce lets loose with a pun or two,
While carrots share secrets, all juicy and new.

Petals of Imagination

Once a daffodil dreamed of a hat,
While a rose cooed sweetly, 'What of that?'
They fashioned their hats from old skies and dew,
And twirled in the wind, feeling fresh and new.

The tulips giggled over their shoes,
Made from petals in bright, quirky hues.
As bees buzzed by, they joined in the play,
With laughter that danced the afternoon away.

Breaths of Creation

A cactus once sighed with a prickly breath,
"Oh, how I wish to escape from my heft!"
It dreamed of a breeze and a gentle sway,
While pondering life, in its spiky way.

The ferns whispered quotes like leaves in the air,
Reciting old sonnets, quite light and rare.
The vines wrapped around and joined in the fun,
Creating a riddle — who said puns can't run?

Fables in the Fields

In fields full of tales where the daisies roam,
A squirrel once scribbled a verse in its home.
It told of a cat with a peculiar quirk,
Who wore mismatched socks, truly proud of its work.

A scarecrow laughed, with a grin so wide,
As he listened to fables from his leafy side.
Sharing tales under a wide-open sky,
With humor like seeds, they let their words fly.

Cultivating Stanzas

In a garden of letters, I plant my lines,
Watering them gently with giggles and pines.
Some sprout into sonnets, while others just tease,
Tickled by breezes, they dance with such ease.

With trowels of humor, I dig deep and wide,
Each word is a seed that I gleefully guide.
The blooms of my verses are silly and bright,
Making laughter grow stronger, like day turns to night.

Roots of Rhyme

Watch as the roots tangle, twist, and unwind,
Finding the punchlines, so perfectly timed.
With rhymes that can giggle and puns that can bop,
These roots hold the secrets of every great drop.

Beneath the soft soil, a happy verse waits,
With phrases that wobble like funny plate weights.
As they reach for the sun, they wiggle and jive,
Creating a garden where laughter's alive.

Flourishing Thoughts

In a patch of wild wit, my musings do thrive,
They stretch and they leap, like a bee on a dive.
With thoughts that are lively, they bloom in a whirl,
Each petal a punchline that makes the mind twirl.

I sprinkle some laughter, a dash of delight,
And watch as they grow under moon's gentle light.
These jovial blooms fill the air with pure glee,
Tickling the senses, just like bumblebees.

Echoes in the Garden

Amidst the tall sunflowers, echoes of cheer,
Whispering jokes that everyone can hear.
The vines weave their tales, with a twist and a grin,
While dandelion wishes float gently in.

The breeze carries laughter from plant to the tree,
As rhymes sprout like daisies, so carefree and free.
In this garden of giggles, the sun gives a nod,
Creating a landscape that's funny and odd.

Tending to the Muse

In a garden where ideas sprout,
I dance 'round weeds, giving a shout.
The muse tickles my brain, oh what a tease,
She jumps like a frog, making me sneeze.

I water my thoughts with laughter and cheer,
Giggling at puns that grow wild here.
Fertilizing rhymes with a sprinkle of fun,
Watch as my silly lines burst like the sun.

Soils of Inspiration

The ground is rich with thoughts so absurd,
Composting dreams, oh haven't you heard?
I plant the odd seeds, some sprout and some flop,
But those quirky blossoms? They never stop!

With shovels for digging and hats made of rhyme,
I wander through lines, oh what a good time!
The worms roll their eyes as I sing to the bugs,
While each silly phrase gives my heart joyful hugs.

Harvesting Dreams

With baskets in hand, I skip through the field,
Gathering giggles, my fate is revealed.
Each chuckle and snort, I pick straight and true,
The punchlines are ripe, with a splash of the blue.

The reaping can be quite a chaotic affair,
As laughter spills out and fills up the air.
Oh, what a harvest, these jokes in a cart,
A feast for my soul, it's a whimsical art!

The Nature of Words

Words flutter like butterflies, colors so bright,
They land on my tongue and take off in flight.
With giggles like petals, they dance in the breeze,
Tickling my senses as they aim to please.

They clump and they tumble, a word salad mix,
Oh, the nonsense can twist like a set of good tricks.
But with joy in my heart, and a wink in my eye,
I toss out my lines like confetti to fly.

Fertile Ground for Ideas

In the garden where thoughts sprout,
Ideas bounce, wiggle, and shout.
A seedling grins, with sunshine bright,
Saying, 'Today, let's take flight!'

We water dreams with zany glee,
Dancing weeds join the jubilee.
A flower winks, just for fun,
Joking, 'I'm now number one!'

Bugs munch on logic, munching slow,
But who cares? We're stealing the show!
In this patch of comedy's play,
We'll plant our quirks and laugh all day.

Germinate a chuckle or two,
What's sprouting now? Perhaps a clue.
In this field, nothing's too absurd,
Where laughter blossoms, all is stirred!

Branches of Reflection

A tree of thoughts sways in the breeze,
Whispering secrets with cheeky ease.
Its branches twist in a comical way,
Saying, 'Life's just a silly ballet!'

Leaves tweet jokes as they flutter down,
While squirrels wear a thoughtful frown.
'Why did the acorn cross the lane?'
'To be a tree, of course! It's plain!'

And shadows play tricks, drawing laughs,
As sunlight tickles the tree's tall halves.
Mirror, mirror on the bark,
Who's the funniest in the park?

With each reflective giggle and sigh,
A breeze of laughter will reply.
So join this tree, for laughs unwind,
In nature's wit, together we'll find!

The Dance of the Seasons

Spring hops in with a jolly twist,
Breezy jokes that you can't resist.
Flowers shimmy, and bees do swing,
'It's a wild party! Come join the fling!'

Summer's here with a sunburned face,
Chasing shadows in a frantic race.
'Why does the sun never get cold?'
'Because it's always too hot to be bold!'

Autumn waves with a leafy cheer,
Pumpkins juggle as Halloween nears.
'Falling leaves are just skits, you see?'
'In this season of humor, we're all free!'

Winter shuffles in with a snowy grin,
Snowflakes giggle, let the fun begin.
While snowmen chuckle with frosty charm,
Spreading joy with their wintery arms!

Blossoms of the Mind

Thoughts bud with a burst of delight,
In the garden, they sprout overnight.
With petals of wisdom, bright and bold,
Each idea a fairy tale told.

A daisy giggles, 'What's in a name?'
'Just a label for this silly game!'
And every flower, a curious spy,
Peeking to see who'll fly or cry.

Ivy climbs on the walls of wit,
Telling stories that just won't quit.
With a vine of laughter, tangled tight,
Twisting language, oh what a sight!

In this fertile patch of comic grace,
We dawdle and dance, a joyous race.
For every bloom holds a quirk so fine,
In the garden of stories, we freely entwine!

Roots of Reflection

In a garden where thoughts grow,
A worm tells jokes, puts on a show.
The daisies giggle, they can't hold tight,
While sunflowers dance, such a silly sight.

A cactus whispers, sharp and sly,
"I'm spiky, but look, I still can fly!"
With roots that wiggle and waddle around,
The laughter echoes, such joy is found.

Cultivation of the Mind

Planting ideas, seeds so bright,
A radish hopes to take flight.
With carrots sporting high-top shoes,
They strut their stuff, so proud, and snooze.

A pickle dreams of being sweet,
Oh dear, what a pickle of a feat!
The lettuce shouts, "I'm romaine!"
As giggles scatter in the grain.

Gentle Wishes on the Breeze

A dandelion makes a wish,
"Oh, for a friend who's not a fish!"
The breeze replies with a chuckle deep,
"I'll scatter you far, no need for sleep!"

A tumbleweed starts to twirl,
"I'm just rolling, what a whirl!"
With whispers floating, soft and light,
The laughter dances, pure delight.

Poetic Blooms

Roses sing of love and cheer,
But violets roll their eyes, oh dear!
The tulips joke and sway with glee,
"Buds up high, can you hear me?"

A sunflower shouts, "I'm the star!"
"Just don't forget, they're here and far!"
As petals toss their heads in fun,
Each bloom a jest, a smile begun.

Leafing Through Lines

In a garden of words we play,
Sowing silly puns all day.
Lines sprout up with little care,
Tickling minds with breaths of air.

Pages flutter, plants unwind,
Doodles dancing, oh so blind.
A raindrop of laughter, a sunbeam's glow,
Who knew lines could grow like a row of crow?

Every stanza, a quirky seed,
Planted in thoughts, yes indeed!
From silly rhymes, fresh fruits appear,
Snack on verses, they bring good cheer.

So leaf through these lines, do not delay,
Taste the silliness, come what may.
With roots in humor, we'll bloom and weave,
In this patch of verse, we all believe!

The Fertile Quill

With a quill that's spry and bright,
I scribble truths that feel just right.
In the soil of mishaps, I dig deep,
Planting giggles that spark and leap.

Words wriggle like worms in a line,
Chortling softly, oh so fine.
With each scratch and scratch, I cultivate,
A harvest of chuckles that can't wait.

An ink pot filled with comical schemes,
Dreams that sprout like wacky beams.
Watered with laughter and sun through the vines,
This fertile quill grows whimsical signs.

So grab your quill, give it a whirl,
Let your laughter twist and twirl.
In this garden where nonsense lies,
The more we giggle, the higher we rise!

Inked Roots

Beneath the soil, ideas take root,
Twisting and turning, oh what a hoot!
With ink that drips like lazy streams,
Growing wild in the land of dreams.

Each phrase a sprout, each pun a shoot,
A hilarious garden, oh so cute!
We dig our fingers into the mess,
Laughing at lines that we can't suppress.

The wiggle of words in soft, rich loam,
Creating a forest we can call home.
With twisted tales and jumbled schemes,
Our inked roots thrive under moonlit beams.

So come along for a hilarious spree,
Where silly words grow wild and free.
In the patch we call ours, let's confide,
With inked roots, let's enjoy the ride!

Verdant Verses

In hues of green, our verses sprout,
Full of jests and giggles, no doubt.
They curl like vines in playful ways,
A comedy garden where laughter plays.

Roots entwined with giggles and grins,
Each line a seed where humor begins.
Nature's giggle in every rhyme,
Growing bright ideas, one verse at a time.

Join this dance of rhythm and cheer,
Where silliness blooms year after year.
Sprinkled with joy, our stanzas grow,
In this verdant patch, we steal the show.

So gather 'round for a jolly good time,
In this garden of jest, we feel sublime.
With verdant verses that twist and twine,
Let's cultivate laughter, oh how divine!

Writing in Full Bloom

Words sprout like daisies, oh so bright,
They dance in the breeze, a comical sight.
Puns and giggles, they twist and twine,
Creating a garden where humor can shine.

With each little bud, a story unfolds,
Tickling your funny bone, if truth be told.
Verses pop up, like mushrooms in spring,
A riot of laughter that wordsmiths can bring.

Ink flows like sap from a tree,
Crafting odd tales, as strange as can be.
In the sunlight of wit, ideas take flight,
A bloom of absurdity, oh what a delight!

So grab your quill, don't be shy,
Let the comical blooms rise up to the sky.
In this garden of giggles, we'll plant all our dreams,
And harvest the chuckles, like sunlit beams.

Enchanted Growth

In a forest of phrases, the laughter is thick,
Where words sprout and stretch, oh what a trick!
A pun here, a jest there, they blossom and grow,
Tickling the mind, setting hearts all aglow.

Silly saplings of thought, with roots intertwining,
Bursting with humor, all faces are shining.
Each line is a petal, so fresh and absurd,
Growing wild like weeds, just waiting to be heard.

From the soil of wit, sprigs take a chance,
With a flutter and giggle, they leap in a dance.
A chorus of chuckles, the trees start to sway,
Branches of joy stretching out every way.

So let's plant our seeds in this whimsical space,
Where fun-loving words find their perfect place.
In the garden of laughter, the magic we'll weave,
Crafting a harvest of joy we believe!

Seeds of Expression

In a garden of thoughts, they sprout,
With rhymes that giggle and twist about.
Each line a seed, planted with flair,
Waiting for chuckles to fill the air.

A stanza wiggles, can't keep still,
Tickling the fancy, what a thrill!
With every word, a chuckle grows,
In this patch of laughs, anything goes.

So dig in the dirt, let's plant some fun,
While verses dance in the bright, warm sun.
A little humor, a splash of cheer,
Springs forth laughter, let's give a cheer!

From tiny thoughts, big laughs take flight,
In this playful garden, all feels right.
With smiles as roots, we'll surely thrive,
In fields of giggles, we come alive.

Verses in Bloom

Lines flutter like petals, so bright,
Each giggle a blossom, a sheer delight.
They sway with the breeze, in playful play,
Dancing and spinning, come what may.

Chasing the sun, they reach for the sky,
In a world of whimsy, they dance high.
A joke for a stem, a pun for a leaf,
Sprouting up joy, beyond all belief.

With laughter as pollen, they spread far,
Each chuckle a seed, our shining star.
In gardens of humor, we all take part,
Tilling the soil of the silly heart.

When blooms of absurdity fill the ground,
We harvest the giggles, so joyfully found.
In the patch of delight, let's all consume,
The sweet, silly fruits of verses in bloom.

The Art of Nurturing Lines

Grab a shovel, it's time to dig,
Witty phrases, oh so big!
We'll plant them here, we'll plant them well,
In this garden where humor excels.

A sprinkle of laughter, a dash of glee,
Watch as the puns grow wild and free.
With a sprinkle and maybe some cheer,
We'll cultivate joy, year after year.

Each verse a seedling, growing stout,
In rows of smiles, there's never a doubt.
Water with chuckles, sunshine with glee,
Nurturing lines, come grow with me!

From little jokes, big stories take flight,
In this funny farm, everything's bright.
So come with your laughter, don't be shy,
Let's harvest some giggles, you and I!

Whispers Under the Canopy

Beneath leaves of laughter, secrets sneak,
Soft whispers of jokes that we all seek.
Tickling the branches, the giggles spread,
In this lively place, that's where we tread.

Silly shadows dance upon the ground,
While the tickle of puns is all around.
Under this canopy, let's all unite,
In a web of joy, so warm and bright.

Whispers of wit float through the air,
Riddles and jests, an absurd affair.
With every rustle, a laugh is made,
Under the trees, our worries fade.

So gather 'round friends, let's revel here,
In this funny grove, let's pump our cheer.
With each silly quip, let's raise a toast,
To laughter and joy, the things we love most.

Words in the Wind

A word once got lost on a breeze,
It tickled the leaves of the trees.
With a giggle it danced, oh so spry,
Chasing the clouds in a bright, blue sky.

A squirrel heard it and started to laugh,
It twirled in circles, a wordy gaffe.
In the garden, it made quite a fuss,
Until a butterfly said, "What's the rush?"

Then a bee chimed in with a buzzing hum,
Saying, "Words are so sweet, like honeycomb!"
They floated together, with rhythm and rhyme,
Creating a buzz that was simply sublime.

So next time you whisper to grass and to air,
Remember the jest that may linger there.
For words have a way of their own merry tune,
Taking flight with the wind like a bright, round balloon.

Seasons of Stanza

In spring, the verses bloom with cheer,
Each line sprouting leaves, oh so clear.
The flowers join in with a colorful shout,
While the rain drops tap dance, no doubt about.

Summer sun blazes, words sizzle and pop,
They swim in a pool, making ripples that drop.
With laughter and giggles, the stanzas grow wild,
As poets get sunburned, all manic and styled.

Then comes autumn, with leaves all aglow,
Lines whisper secrets as breezes do blow.
The pumpkins all chuckle, their jokes on display,
While the harvest of verses just drips with bouquet.

Winter's cold touch wraps the pages in white,
A snowflake of silence, oh what a sight!
Yet still, through the frost, rhythms twirl and glide,
In seasons of laughter, there's joy to reside.

Lines Among the Lilies

Among the lilies, a quip did arise,
A line full of giggles, much to our surprise.
With petals so bright, they started to sway,
As if they could hear every word that we say.

A frog croaked a sonnet, or maybe a tune,
That echoed through gardens, beneath the moon.
The lilacs all chuckled, the daisies joined in,
As rhymes bounced around like a whimsical spin.

A bumblebee buzzed, carrying verse
With pollen for metaphors cleverly terse.
He landed on flowers, then promptly forgot,
Only to hum what the garden begot.

Then came a cat with a flick of its tail,
Prowling through poetry, leaving a trail.
With a wink and a grin, it joined in the play,
As lines among lilies danced night into day.

Nature's Inkpot

In nature's own inkpot, where rivers run dry,
A quill made of feathers danced up to the sky.
It dipped in the ocean, and wrote on the sand,
Creating new verses where fun meets the grand.

The mountains all giggled, their echoes were bright,
As clouds turned to paper, in soft, fluffy light.
With each fleeting shadow, a line took its flight,
A poem in motion, a pure delight.

The winds carried whispers of cacti so wise,
Who penned down their secrets, much to our surprise.
Each cactus a poet, bold and with glee,
Spinning tales of the desert in vibrant spree.

So next time you wander through branches and leaves,
Let nature's inkpot fill all your believes.
For words are the seeds, they spring up and grow,
In this funny old world, letting laughter flow.

Beneath the Surface

In the garden of laughs, seeds are sown,
With giggles as water, they're beautifully grown.
A pun in the soil, a joke on the vine,
They sprout in the sunlight, so silly, divine.

Worms wiggle and chuckle, they dance underground,
While daisies tell stories in petals profound.
The roots intertwine as secrets they share,
In this wacky tableau, we're all in midair.

Frogs leap from their pads, in suits made of leaves,
Reciting their rhymes, while the whole garden heaves.
The flowers all burst with laughter in bloom,
In this jolly patch, let's make room for the zoom.

So next time you stroll through the greenery bright,
Just listen for chuckles between day and night.
Each giggle a petal, each snicker a sprout,
In the comedy show that life's all about.

Landscapes of Emotion

In fields of wild humor, the sun shines so loud,
With laughter as clouds, we're a fun-loving crowd.
Each tear maybe silly, or sweet as a plum,
In the meadows of smiles, we all come undone.

The hills are alive with the sound of a snort,
While butterflies dance in their whimsical court.
With whispers of chuckles tracing paths through the air,
They tickle our senses, without any care.

Rainstorms of giggles can wash worries away,
With puddles of joy where the children can play.
Each squishy footstep gives birth to a laugh,
In this landscape of humor, we'll always have half.

A mountain of memories, each climb brings a cheer,
With mates by our side, there's nothing to fear.
So let's keep creating this colorful view,
In this vast tapestry, there's room for the crew.

Vines of Connection

Twisting and turning, the jokes entwine,
In circles of laughter, all hearts realign.
With quirky connections hanging from the trees,
The air is a canvas, bustling with glee.

Like ivy that curls and embraces the wall,
Our punchlines all tangle, the humor won't fall.
The roots run so deep, in this forest of fun,
Where vines of good words grow warmer than sun.

With snickers and titter, the branches expand,
As echoes of fun scatter across the land.
Each leaf holds a secret, a chuckle to share,
In this verdant embrace, we forget all our care.

And as we climb higher in this leafy spree,
Every tickle of laughter, a moment set free.
So hug those tight vines and let laughter bind,
In this garden of whimsy, we truly unwind.

Tides of Expression

Waves of bright chuckles crash on the shore,
As seagulls retell what the surf has in store.
Each splash a new line, a moment so grand,
In this ocean of wit, we all take a stand.

The moon pulls our laughter like tides on the sand,
While jellyfish giggle as they sway hand in hand.
With shells that hold stories, each grin takes a bow,
In this sea of expression, we're anchored somehow.

The surfboards of humor ride high on the crest,
While dolphins sneak glances, so quickly impressed.
With seaweed as punchlines, they dance to the beat,
In this aquatic world, life feels so sweet.

And when the day fades, with a wink from the sun,
We gather our tales, oh what silly fun!
Let's share all our laughter, till the stars dance above,
In these tides of expression, we find what we love.

Blossoming Dreams

In a garden where giggles bloom,
Flowers wear hats, dispelling gloom.
Roses whisper jokes, oh what a scene,
Tulips dance like they've never seen.

Bees buzz around, cracking puns,
While daisies roll in the morning sun.
A sunflower winks, quite bold and bright,
Nature's humor, a sheer delight.

Petals float, like silly notes,
Singing praises, in joyful throats.
With each new sprout, laughter grows,
Sharing secrets beneath the rows.

Breezes chuckle, clouds chime in,
A whimsical world where grins begin.
Find the mirth in every scene,
In this garden, where dreams are green.

The Blossomed Page

In a book where flowers write,
Words hop around in pure delight.
Pages rustle, they laugh and play,
Crafting tales in a silly way.

The daisies tell of sunny days,
While violets share mischievous ways.
Pencils bloom with laughter's cheer,
As colors splash, drawing near.

Chapters grow like tangled vines,
Plot twists shown in whimsical lines.
A lily pens a joke or two,
While hyacinths giggle and skew.

So flip the page, let the fun unfold,
In the garden of stories, bright and bold.
A tale of blooms, laughter's embrace,
The joyful journey, an endless chase.

Cultured Imagery

Brushes dip in hues so spry,
Painting smiles that float and fly.
Strawberries scatter thoughts anew,
While broccoli thinks it's quite the view.

Canvases laugh, splattered with gold,
Each stroke a tale, a secret told.
Artichokes pose with flair and grace,
While carrots giggle in their place.

Palette dances, a merry swirl,
As colors merge in a playful twirl.
From daisies' quotes to leafy lines,
A vibrant world where whimsy shines.

So paint your dreams with joy and jest,
In this garden, let fun manifest.
Craft your vision, let laughter lead,
With cultured imagery, we all succeed!

Nature's Wordsmith

A squirrel types on acorns bright,
Crafting tales of day and night.
With every nibble, stories flow,
In a woodland nook, where laughter grows.

Birds compose with chirps and tweets,
Creating sonnets on sunny streets.
A raccoon edits with a cheeky grin,
Turning mischief into wins.

Letters tumble from leafy trees,
As nature giggles with gentle breeze.
Each word a seed, sprouting delight,
In this forest, humor takes flight.

So gather 'round, join the fun,
In the wordsmith's world, we're all one.
With stories shared, let laughter claim,
Nature's charm, a joyful game.

The Garden of Stanzas

In a bright plot where words sprout,
They dance around like seeds of doubt.
Pronouns giggle, nouns take flight,
Puns bloom boldly, what a sight!

Adjectives frolic in the grass,
While verbs race by, oh what a class!
The jokes grow tall, the rhymes entwine,
In this garden, all is fine!

Each line a leaf, all fresh and spry,
Commas wander, while periods fly.
Metaphors climb up the fence,
Tickling thoughts, so many scents!

In the soil of wit, we dig so deep,
Harvesting giggles, laughter to reap.
In our patch of jests, we careen,
Nature's humor, so fresh and green!

Words Beneath the Canopy

Underneath the leafy shade,
Silly phrases start to invade.
Whispering jokes to the gentle breeze,
Tickling thoughts, just like teasing bees.

A pun lands softly on my head,
As giggles ripple, and we're misled.
A homophone slips on the grass,
What a mess! Can't let that pass!

Riddles hiding in the roots,
Playful stanzas in bright suits.
With every breeze, the laughter grows,
Funny tales, as the sunlight glows.

Beneath the canopy so wide,
Jokes sprout up from every side.
In this forest of witty charms,
We find humor that disarms!

Branching Narratives

On branches thick with tales to tell,
Words hang ripe, like fruit from a well.
Each story swings, a comedy ride,
As punchlines soar and take a slide.

Boughs that twist and turn with glee,
Where metaphors thrive, wild and free.
Plot thickens like a stew in a pot,
Where laughter brews, and smiles are caught.

A narrative walks the tightrope high,
Juggling puns as the birds fly by.
Characters leap from leaf to leaf,
Sprouting laughter, joy, and belief.

Under the canopy of quirky lore,
Each twist and turn, we do explore.
Branching out with stories galore,
With every giggle, we seek more!

Inked Petals

In the garden of words, oh how they bloom,
With inked petals consuming the room.
Each stanza a flower, spritzed with prose,
A whiff of humor, as laughter grows.

Doodles dance on the page, so bright,
Characters burst, day turns to night.
The verses flutter, like butterflies,
Turning chuckles into sweet sighs.

Blossoms inked in comedy's hue,
With petals of thoughts, fresh and new.
Each line a sprig of wild delight,
Chasing the shadows, igniting light.

In this patch where silliness reigns,
The jokes pop up like sweet sugar canes.
Inked petals bloom, oh what a delight,
A garden of giggles, a joyful sight!

Lyrical Landscapes

In a field where rhymes can grow,
Worms write sonnets in the soil below.
Each line they wiggle, each verse they sprawl,
Nature's giggles echo, oh what a brawl!

The daisies dance, a balletic affair,
While a squirrel recites without a care.
They tumble and trip, the bees join in,
Sipping sweet honey, they're all in the spin!

A rainbow of lines, splashed here and there,
The clouds are envious, but they don't dare.
A poet sneezes, and the words take flight,
Fluffy like cotton candy, pure delight!

So let's sip our tea, with rhymes that stick,
In this garden of giggles, where silliness ticks.
Each stanza sprouts funny, like weeds in a row,
In landscapes of laughter, let the verses flow!

Nature's Canvas

Colors collide on a bright summer day,
The trees wear hats, in a whimsical way.
A brush with the breeze paints giggles anew,
As flowers plot mischief, who knew they could do?

Bees in tuxedos buzz around with flair,
Pollen as confetti, floating in the air.
A caterpillar drafts an ode on a leaf,
To a butterfly's dance—a hilarious motif!

Clouds are the audience, they laugh in delight,
As the sunsets toss colors, a comical sight.
With a wink and a nod, the moon joins the fun,
Under this canvas, the laughing's not done!

Stars chime in sprightly, like a jingle at night,
A chorus of twinkles, a riot of light.
Every giggle is painted, every chuckle immense,
On Nature's big canvas, where joy is the sense!

Ink and Ivy

Inking my thoughts on a vine-covered wall,
The ivy spreads tales of humourous fall.
As leaves whisper secrets, I chuckle along,
In this tricky garden, I'm writing a song!

A snail recites verses at a glacial pace,
While ants in tuxedos all join the race.
With every little stride, giggles ripple through,
The pen starts to wobble, it's tickling too!

Roses roll their eyes, such drama unfolds,
Their petals are gossip, oh the stories they hold.
A worm with a quill jots down all the fuss,
Labeling the chaos, "An inky plus!"

So let's raise a cup to this ivy-clad place,
Where humor's a vine, twining swift with grace.
Ink spills like laughter, sharing joy on its way,
In the heart of each scribble, let's giggle and play!

Growth in Metaphor

Deep in the garden of whimsical thought,
Metaphors dance, all tangled and caught.
A sunflower giggles, reaching for the sky,
Chasing clouds that tease and flit on by.

Trees tell tall tales of their journeys long,
Barking out punchlines with roots that are strong.
The grass does the waving, quite joyful and sly,
Tickling the toes of those walking by.

A pumpkin proclaims, "I'm funny and bright!"
While carrots break into a veggie delight.
The beets share laughs in a rooty embrace,
In this patch of puns, it's a comical space!

So let shovels dig deep for a laugh underground,
In this garden of growth, where humor's profound.
Let joy sprout in lines, with a wink at the sun,
In the metaphor farm, we're all here for fun!

Tales from the Orchard

In a garden where nonsense grows,
Silly seeds sprout, who knows?
Tomatoes wearing funny hats,
Dance with chickens, chat with rats.

Pears play tag, oranges will trip,
Lemons form a comedy skit.
Bees buzz tunes, buzz buzz get loud,
While squirrels prance, oh how proud!

Grapes throw parties, hang around,
Mangoes roll and tumble down.
Every corner, laughter ripe,
Who knew fruit could be such hype?

So stroll through this jolly grove,
Find the joy that fruits can prove.
In the orchard, laughter's found,
A fruity joke that laughs abound.

Cultivating Thoughts

In minds where wild ideas roam,
Watch them sprout, make thoughts their home.
A seedling slips on a thought cap,
Bouncing ideas like a funny chap.

Giggles take root, ideas entwine,
Dancing like veggies on a vine.
Carrots sing, beans join the play,
Oh, how joyful thoughts can sway!

We plant our worries in the ground,
Pulling laughter from the sound.
Rooftops filled with quirky dreams,
Slipping on thoughts like silly streams.

So dig your hands in, don't be shy,
Let's grow giggles up to the sky.
Fertile minds are silly sights,
Where laughter blooms and takes flight.

Leaves of Inspiration

Leaves twirl down in a dance so weird,
Whispering jokes that we've all feared.
Each green bit holds a witty line,
Nature's laughter, simply divine.

Flat leaves speak of wishes unheard,
While pointy ones chatter absurd.
In the breeze they twist and spin,
Gather 'round, let the fun begin!

Rustling tales of sun and rain,
Each drop a pun, or so they claim.
A comedy show in the treetops bright,
Leaves of humor, a delightful sight!

So relish in nature's leafy jest,
Where laughter grows, it's simply the best.
In sunny glades and shady nooks,
Find the fun in storybooks.

Roots of Rhyme

Down in the dirt where giggles dwell,
Roots weave tales that tickle so well.
Buried puns in tangled threads,
Whispers of laughter beneath our beds.

Wiggly roots share secrets deep,
Funny stories that never sleep.
Kaleidoscope of whimsy and jest,
Underneath, they plan a fest!

When the ground shakes, it's a great cheer,
Roots erupt with grins, oh dear!
Spaghetti vines twist with glee,
Claiming crowns as the kings of spree.

So dig a little and let it flow,
Let roots take part in the humor show.
Beneath the surface, joy will bloom,
In the earth, there's laughter room.

The Chorus of Dawn

The sun yawns wide, with a stretch and a grin,
While birds gather round, let the nonsense begin.
They sing a tune, whimsical and bright,
Echoing laughter, from morning to night.

A rooster joins in, with a crow and a flap,
As the coffee pot brews for a morning mishap.
The blossoms all giggle, not one is aloof,
Painting the day like a playful goof.

The dew drops dance, on petals so round,
In the merry garden, where joy can be found.
With veggies and flowers, a colorful spree,
They chuckle in chorus, just you wait and see!

So if you hear giggles, at the break of day,
It's just nature's party, come join in the play.
With blooms sprouting jokes, and sunshine on cue,
The morning's a stage, we're all actors too!

From Dust to Bloom

In a patch of dirt, a seed took a nap,
Dreaming of sunlight and a leafy cap.
With a wiggle and wiggle, oh what a show!
Dust turned to laughter, and up it did grow.

A worm whispered secrets, in the cool earth bed,
Tales of the sky and the colors red.
The seed peeped out, with a bold little sprout,
Chasing the giggles, it couldn't pout.

A raindrop came down, with a comedic splash,
Turning the garden into a water bash.
The flowers all danced, as the seeds would plume,
From dust to delight, just look how they bloom!

So next time you find, a patch with no view,
Remember the giggles that come from the blue.
For each little seed, has a story to tell,
Of laughter and flowers, all thriving so well!

Seeds of Verses

A tiny seed landed, with a wish in its core,
To sprout into lines, that the bees would adore.
With the sun as its pen, and the wind as the muse,
It scribbled sweet whims, in delightful hues.

It tickled the daisies, made them giggle out loud,
Created a ruckus, in the leafy crowd.
Each petal a quote, each bud a new line,
Spreading the joy, like a well-aged wine.

The sunflowers danced, they were part of the game,
Reciting soft verses, never sounding the same.
With bees as the audience, buzzing with glee,
They reveled together, in sweet harmony.

So if you see a garden, full of cheer and play,
Know the seeds are crafting, their poetic ballet.
Just listen real close, as they play with the breeze,
For in every small sprout, lives a tale that'll please!

Whispering Blossoms

In the corner garden, whispers take flight,
From buds and blooms, sharing secrets so bright.
They giggle and jive, with petals a-flutter,
As bumblebees join, making sweet, silly clutter.

A daisy confided, in a voice so discreet,
'The tulips are plotting a grand flower treat!'
With colors a-chatter, they all shared a wink,
As the marigolds laughed, 'Drink nectar, don't think!'

Every blossom had stories, of sun and of rain,
Of growing and thriving, and even of pain.
Yet laughter was woven in each fragrant sigh,
As they turned every tear into jokes on the fly.

So next time you wander, through gardens of glee,
Listen closely, and you might just agree.
For blossoms are whispers, they giggle in bloom,
Filling the world with a bright floral room!

Fables of Flora

The daisies dance with glee,
While the tulips flip their hair.
A cactus throws a party,
Without a worry or a care.

The roses tell a joke,
While the violets roll their eyes.
The daisies chime in laughter,
Underneath the sunny skies.

The sunflowers seek tall tales,
While the ferns are feeling shy.
A gopher cracks a pun,
And all the bulbs reply, 'Oh my!'

With petals glowing brightly,
And roots that reach so far,
The garden's one big laugh fest,
Underneath the twinkling star.

The Harvest of Dreams

Carrots sport their orange coats,
As corn takes up the spot.
The peas make silly faces,
With pods that giggle a lot.

Pumpkins roll in funny ways,
And squash just likes to play.
They hop around the field,
In a very veggie ballet.

Tomatoes burst with laughter,
As radishes shake in rhyme.
The onions hold their breath,
In the silliest of times.

With every silly harvest,
They cheer, "What a great crop!"
In this famished field of fun,
Where giggles never stop.

Rhymes Under the Sun

The butterflies are rhyming,
In the meadow's sunny glow.
They twist, they spin, they flutter,
Like poets on a show.

The ladybugs are clapping,
To the beat of buzzing bees.
While grasshoppers recite lines,
Swaying on the breezes.

A squirrel drops a rhyme,
That makes the tree trunks quake.
The flowers nod their heads,
As the giggling stems awake.

Underneath the bright blue sky,
With every cheerful pun,
The rhythm in the garden,
Is a laugh for everyone.

Waves of Green Sentiment

The broccoli is pondering,
In the garden's sunny flair.
With thoughts of how to dance,
In its veggie-loving hair.

The lettuce joins in chorus,
With a crunch that's oh so bold.
While peppers sing their zesty tunes,
In shades of red and gold.

The beans begin a jig,
In a sway that's quite a sight.
While every vine is giggling,
From morning until night.

With laughter growing louder,
In this jungle of delight,
The garden waves together,
In a funny, vibrant light.

Tending the Heart's Garden

In the plot of my heart, I plant little seeds,
Watering dreams and some silly deeds.
With a sprinkle of laughter and bright sunshine,
I tend to these quirks, and they all turn divine.

Weeds of worry try to take hold,
But I chuckle them out, being bold and sold.
Composting woes, a rich fertilizer,
My garden blooms bright, a true energizer.

With care and with humor, I prune with delight,
Leaving room for the giggles that dance in the light.
Each blossom a memory, quirky and grand,
They're the smiles of my heart, scattered like sand.

So plant a few puns in the soil of your mind,
Let laughter come forth, don't leave it behind.
For in this wild garden, let joy take its turn,
For every good chuckle, there's more to be learned.

Flourished Expressions

Words in the air, like balloons on a spree,
Floating around, come dance with me.
A wink and a pun, they grow very tall,
With laughter as sunlight, they won't let you fall.

Tickles of syntax turn into a beast,
Spreading their humor and yet craving a feast.
For every lost comma, there's joy to be found,
In the silliness looming all around.

Each verse a sprout, some poking out right,
Chuckling and wobbling, a marvelous sight.
So gather these phrases, let's plant them in rows,
A harvest of giggles, where silliness grows.

With bright, quirky flowers and charm built to last,
These expressions will flourish, far outgrowing the past.
So let's cultivate joy, both silly and fun,
In gardens of laughter, where we've only begun.

Branches of Thought

Thoughts branch out wildly, like trees in full bloom,
Some crooked and quirky, they chase after gloom.
With each twist and turn, they tickle and tease,
Inviting sweet chuckles carried by the breeze.

I prune my ideas, snip the old fears,
With scissors of laughter, and a dash of cheers.
The bark of my ponderings, rough but secure,
Shields me from woes, that's for sure!

Leaves flutter like jokes, catching sunbeams so bright,
Each one a reminder to giggle at night.
As branches reach out, they create quite a mess,
Yet in all this chaos, I find happiness.

So swing on these branches, let your thoughts fly,
No leaf left unturned, from ground to the sky.
For funny ideas, they always make space,
In the wild woods of wonder, there's room for embrace.

Words Take Root

Words take a dive in the soil of my mind,
With a twist of the tongue, they're all intertwined.
Each phrase a shoot, poking up through the ground,
Sprouting up joy that is waiting around.

Some pop up like daisies, all friendly and bright,
While others wear puns, making hilarity's height.
Their roots sink in deep, shooting laughter up high,
I'm farming for giggles, oh me, oh my!

I water my verses, sprinkle cheer on the bed,
Pruning back worries, no need to dread.
A bouquet of laughter in full bloom I see,
Words whispering secrets, come laugh along with me.

So dig deep in your thoughts, let the humor unfurl,
Let your heart blossom, and give it a twirl.
With each quirk and rhyme, watch your joy explode,
Harvesting fun on this whimsical road.

Tangled Verses

In a garden of words, a tangle of vines,
Sentences twist like drunken designs.
Adjectives dance, with verbs on the run,
A pun in the petunias, oh what fun!

Nouns wear wigs, while adverbs stroll,
In the playground of phrases, they've lost control.
Metaphors tumble, with giggles they fall,
A circus of language, we're having a ball!

Roses of rhythm and daisies of rhyme,
Compose a bouquet; it's storytime!
Yet in all this mess, we find a delight,
A kaleidoscope of nonsense shines bright!

So let's plant some laughter, a plot on the side,
With giggles as fertilizer, let humor abide.
The garden of voices has grown quite a lot,
In this tangled adventure, forget-me-not!

Sunlit Pages

On sunlit pages, where thoughts do parade,
Scribbles and doodles in rhymes masquerade.
A comical tale of a shoe and a cat,
They dance in the sunshine; imagine that!

With laughter like rays, they bounce off the walls,
A paper airplane that giggles and falls.
The ink splashes joy with each playful stroke,
In this tale of absurd, not once did we choke!

From a sunbeam's grin to the shadows' surprise,
Witty wordplay makes us chuckle and rise.
The sun dips low, but we're still in the light,
Our pages are glowing; what a fine sight!

So gather your verses, let the laughter flow,
With each scribbled line, let the silliness grow.
In the warmth of the sun, where the giggles ignite,
We celebrate words till the fall of the night!

Vibrant Echoes

In the valley of giggles, where echoes collide,
Jokes bounce like bunnies, and soon they will glide.
The punchline's a trampoline, springing us high,
Laughter cascades like a giddy goodbye!

Synonyms hop like frogs in a rush,
As similes bubble, creating a hush.
In the chorus of chuckles, we find our refrain,
With each vibrant echo, we giggle again!

Onomatopoeia sings, with a pop and a bang,
While limericks leap in a joyful slang.
The harmony sways like a leaf in the breeze,
In this festive soundscape, our worries appease.

So let's share a laugh in this lyrical park,
Where humor and rhyme leave an unmistakable mark.
With vibrant echoes ringing, we jubilantly cheer,
For the joy of the jest will always be near!

The Weaving of Words

Once I woke up in a hammock of verse,
Dreams tangled with metaphors, nothing was terse.
I spun a delight from a spool of bright line,
And tied it together with humor divine!

In the loom of the day, I stitched up a pun,
With laughter as thread, so ideas could run.
My tapestry glimmers with sparkles and glee,
As the weaver of whimsy, I'm wild and free!

The warp and the weft, a fabric of jest,
Where rhymes take a ride on a feathery quest.
Each stitch a giggle, each knot a good cheer,
The canvas of laughter is perfectly clear!

So come, take a dance in this merry design,
In the weaving of words, let your spirit align.
For a life woven brightly with humor and grace,
Is a masterpiece painted in this joyous space!

Flourishing Fantasies

In a garden where giggles sprout,
A thought once whispered turned about.
Tiny seeds of dreams take flight,
Under the sun, they dance with delight.

Butterflies play, wearing hats made of cheese,
While daisies hum tunes that aim to please.
Laughter spills like lemonade,
In this silly world, joys are made.

Worms in bow ties wiggle and writhe,
Painting the soil with mirth to survive.
Each petal tells a joke on a breeze,
Tickling the air, aiming to tease.

So let's plant a patch of whimsical dreams,
Where nothing is ever as simple as it seems.
With each chuckle, a bloom will arise,
In a realm where humor never dies.

Sowing the Imagination

In a patch where ideas grow stout,
We toss out thoughts with a kingly shout.
Each notion lands like a flying fish,
Flipping through air, granting a wish.

Clouds wear socks, and stars roller skate,
As we cultivate dreams, never too late.
The soil is rich with laughter and fun,
Planting oddities under the sun.

We sprinkle some giggles, a dash of surprise,
Watch as the giggling daisies rise.
Fanciful weeds make the silliest stew,
Brewing up magic, a brew just for you.

Nurtured by joy, our garden will thrive,
With each wild thought, we come alive.
So grab a spade, let's dig deep inside,
In this fertile ground, let our hearts collide.

The Heart's Harvest

In a field where chuckles grow tall,
We gather the joy, we gather it all.
Pick a handful of dreams that aren't shy,
And toss them up high to paint the sky.

With baskets of laughter, we skip down the lane,
Collecting the snippets that dance in the rain.
Each giggle a fruit, each grin a delight,
Harvesting moments, under the moonlight.

So dance with the daisies and sing with the bees,
Share all your wit with the fluttering leaves.
Each merry heart beats in rhythm with cheer,
As we sow all our mischief, year after year.

Let's gather the wonders unearthed from our heart,
These bounties of joy, life's greatest art.
With laughter as fertilizer, grow wide and apart,
We'll feast on the magic, a state-of-the-art.

Blossoms of Thought

In a realm where giggles bloom,
Thoughts sprout up, filling the room.
A blink of an eye, a twirl of a thought,
Creates a bouquet of silliness sought.

With each quirky whim, a flower unfolds,
Dressed in colors that never get old.
Tickles of brilliance sway side to side,
In this playful garden, nonsense won't hide.

We sip on ideas, like sipping hot tea,
While mushrooms wear glasses and dance with glee.
Every petal has stories, some funny, some wise,
Transforming the mundane into a surprise.

So let's grow a patch filled with laughter anew,
Where jokes blossom freely, like morning dew.
In the tapestry woven from thoughts of delight,
We'll celebrate every giggle, morning to night.

Threads of the Wild

In a garden of giggles, seeds sprout with glee,
Worms do the tango, so wild and free.
Bumblebees buzzing, wearing tiny hats,
Dancing on daisies, swatting at chitchats.

Squirrels in suits, debating the trees,
With acorn briefcases, nothing to please.
Nature's a circus, with laughs on the run,
Who knew the branches could have so much fun?

Frogs in a frenzy, they croak out their jokes,
And snail races happen with bursts of soft smokes.
A rabbit in glasses quips wise with a grin,
While the sun winks down, the laughter just spins.

Spinning in circles, the leaves swirl around,
Each twist a connection, where smiles abound.
In this playful garden, where quirks intertwine,
Life's a sweet jest, like a vintage red wine.

Cultures of the Canvas

Brushes are chatting, each stroke has its say,
Colors collide in a spectacular play.
Canvas giggles with splashes of cheer,
While paint drips like secrets, what a sight here!

Pencils whisper stories as artists take flight,
Sketching squirrels in mittens, oh what a sight!
The paint pot is laughing, throwing bright hues,
While the canvas grins wide in polka-dot shoes.

Easel's a platform for silliness grand,
Where blobs of blue jellyfish flip on the sand.
With each stroke a giggle, each color a tease,
Art becomes mischief, in twirls, it will please.

Creativity spreads like confetti in air,
Mirthful mishaps—there's joy everywhere!
In this joyful exhibit, the laughter's alive,
Oh, to be part of the colors that thrive!

Fragments in the Breeze

Whispers of laughter flutter on high,
As leaves wear their capes and take to the sky.
Dandelions puff out their fluffy dreams,
Sharing sweet secrets in soft, playful gleams.

Socks in the wind, do pirouettes bold,
While clouds crack up in their puffs of white gold.
The sun throws confetti of warmth in the air,
Tickling the branches, with fun everywhere.

Butterflies bicker in vibrant debates,
Their wings are like stories that dance in the fates.
A breeze brings the giggles of nature at play,
As fragments of whimsy just flutter away.

The horizon is grinning, a sight to behold,
With ripples of laughter in hues bright and bold.
In this whimsical world, there's joy to be found,
As the fragments join hands, twirling round and round.

Songs Beneath the Sun

Under the sun, where the laughter can thrive,
Crickets play tunes that keep dreams alive.
Buttercups giggle, they sway to the beat,
As grasshoppers leap with their tap-dancing feet.

The old willow whispers secrets so spry,
To the daisies who nod, and wink with a sigh.
Each note that they hum, like a tickle in air,
Turns the meadow to magic, a whimsical lair.

Bumblebees trumpet, in chorus so grand,
With flips and with dips, they take a sweet stand.
The sun sings a ballad, so warm and so bright,
While flowers sway gently, in pure delight.

Oh, sing me a symphony, joyous and clear,
With rhythms that echo, like laughter we hear.
For every soft flutter beneath the sky's dome,
Are songs of sweet nature, where all can call home.

The Art of Blossoming

In the garden where laughs take flight,
Petunias giggle in the warm sunlight.
Daisies dance, with sway so divine,
While sunflowers sip tea, feeling fine.

Worms in tuxedos, quite the sight,
Debate the best way to grow overnight.
Bumblebees buzzing, playing a tune,
A harmony made beneath the moon.

The roses are chuckling, full of glee,
As they gossip of bees, and who's a 'he.'
Their petals aflutter, in rhymes and puns,
Filling the air with laughter and fun.

So let's raise a toast to this floral spree,
Where flowers embrace whimsy, wild and free.
In this garden of mirth, we'll joyfully sprout,
Creating a sonnet, there's never a doubt.

Untamed Verses

Words run wild in the open air,
Like dandelions bouncing without a care.
Each syllable springs forth with a smile,
Chasing the butterflies, all the while.

Nonsense in rhythms, a rollicking spree,
Sentences leap, full of glee.
Conversations with crickets, so absurd,
In a symphony crafted, without a word.

Scribbles and giggles, quirks on the page,
As squirrels act out, quite the stage.
Puns tumble like acorns, all over the place,
While rhymes take a silly, frollicking race.

So let your thoughts frolic, set them to roam,
In the whimsical wilderness, you're free to drone.
Embrace the madness, let chaos unfurl,
In the garden of phrases, humor's your pearl.

Fertility of Expression

Ideas sprout like mushrooms in spring,
Each thought a bright, cheerful thing.
They bloom and they flourish, take flight,
In a patchwork of nonsense, pure delight.

Giggles and wiggles, the curls of the pen,
Words tickle the brain like a soft little hen.
Poems are puddles we splash through with glee,
Making a mess, oh, how fun it can be!

Jokes in the margins, all snug and tight,
While rhymes romp around, a pure delight.
Crafting a canvas where thoughts can be free,
Every word carries a splash of esprit.

So dig in the soil of your mind with zest,
Let humor and joy be what you express.
The fruits of your labor, let laughter ensue,
In this garden of fun, there's room for all you.

Whispers Among the Wildflowers

In the field of laughter where daisies confide,
Gentle whispers of joy, a tickle inside.
Butterflies giggle, sharing bright tales,
While the breeze joins in with whimsical gales.

The petals gossip about clouds up above,
Chasing the sun, as they dance and shove.
A joke from the weeds leaves everyone grinning,
As the flowers laugh, oh, this joy's just beginning.

With every swish and sway, the joy multiplies,
Nature's own humor in playful disguise.
Dew drops laugh as they ride on a leaf,
Filling the morning with joy and belief.

So come join the chorus, all creatures and blooms,
Together we'll flourish, dispelling the glooms.
In this meadow of mirth, let glee find its place,
Whispers of joy, in every soft face.

www.ingramcontent.com/pod-product-compliance
Lightning Source LLC
Chambersburg PA
CBHW050304120526
44590CB00016B/2481